The Handy Little Guide to
Lent

THE
HANDY
LITTLE
GUIDE
TO
Lent

Michelle Schroeder

Our Sunday Visitor

Nihil Obstat
Msgr. Michael Heintz, Ph.D.
Censor Librorum

Imprimatur
✠ Kevin C. Rhoades
Bishop of Fort Wayne-South Bend
August 14, 2020

The *Nihil Obstat* and *Imprimatur* are official declarations that a book is free from doctrinal or moral error. It is not implied that those who have granted the *Nihil Obstat* and *Imprimatur* agree with the contents, opinions, or statements expressed.

Except where noted, the Scripture citations used in this work are taken from the *Revised Standard Version of the Bible — Second Catholic Edition* (Ignatius Edition), copyright © 1965, 1966, 2006 National Council of the Churches of Christ in the United States of America. Used by permission. All rights reserved.

English translation of the *Catechism of the Catholic Church* for use in the United States of America copyright © 1994, United States Catholic Conference, Inc. — Libreria Editrice Vaticana. English translation of the *Catechism of the Catholic Church: Modifications from the Editio Typica* copyright © 1997, United States Catholic Conference, Inc. — Libreria Editrice Vaticana.

Every reasonable effort has been made to determine copyright holders of excerpted materials and to secure permissions as needed. If any copyrighted materials have been inadvertently used in this work without proper credit being given in one form or another, please notify Our Sunday Visitor in writing so that future printings of this work may be corrected accordingly.

Copyright © 2020 by Michelle Schroeder

25 24 23 22 21 20   1 2 3 4 5 6 7 8 9

All rights reserved. With the exception of short excerpts for critical reviews, no part of this work may be reproduced or transmitted in any form or by any means whatsoever without permission from the publisher. For more information, visit: www.osv.com/permissions.

Our Sunday Visitor Publishing Division, Our Sunday Visitor, Inc., 200 Noll Plaza, Huntington, IN 46750; 1-800-348-2440; www.osv.com.

ISBN: 978-1-68192-671-1 (Inventory No. T2563)
LCCN: 2020941058

Cover design: Amanda Falk
Cover art: AdobeStock
Interior design: Lindsey Riesen

PRINTED IN THE UNITED STATES OF AMERICA

Contents

Your Penance: Read This Introduction 7

Where's My Alleluia? 11

#ashtag 15

Pump Up the Prayer 19

Almsgiving 23

It's Getting Weird 27

The Lent Survey 31

It's Only Twice a Year (Maybe) 35

But Whyyy??? 39

But I Want It! 45

There's a Catch 49

No Excuses 53

Give It Up and Fast 57

Quick Reminder: Go to Confession! 61

Go for the Trifecta 63

It's Finally Over 67

Your Penance: Read This Introduction

Lent is the season of sackcloth and ashes, hymns that sound like funeral dirges, and a generally heavy feeling that seems to permeate our entire Catholic universe. Sounds awesome, doesn't it? Well, maybe on the surface Lent isn't the most cheerful billboard for our faith, but it is one of the spiritually richest seasons of the liturgical year. Lent is a time when we can truly grow by leaps and bounds in our faith life. Do you want to get the most out of this incredible opportunity for growing in closeness to Christ? Excellent. Then keep reading.

Lent is not merely forty days where we can't eat meat on Fridays and have to give up something we like. According to the *Catechism of the Catholic Church*, "By the solemn forty days of *Lent* the Church unites herself each year to the mystery of Jesus in the desert" (540). In a broader sense, Lent is an invitation to develop a deeper relationship with Jesus.

Lent is about sacrifice, and, yes, giving up candy may actually have something to do with going to heaven. Lent is a time when we think more about our sinfulness, and gloomy as it sounds this practice can actually bring us closer to Jesus. Lent is a time of palpable sadness in the Church, yet that very sadness is meant to lead us to eternal happiness. We'll explore these seeming contradictions in the following pages. We'll also look closely at prayer, fasting (sacrifice), and almsgiving, and how we should approach these things during the Lenten season. The goal here is to better utilize the forty days of Lent to unite more closely with Jesus and grow in love for our Lord.

But shouldn't we be working toward a closer relationship with the Lord all the time, not just during Lent? Yes! But Lent is a particularly good opportunity because as a whole Church, we can more closely journey with Jesus on the cross. We all live with crosses. Whether we're dealing with family stress, financial hardship, illness, or other sufferings, we can all relate in some way to the suffering Jesus endured in his passion and death. But during Lent, the Church's liturgy and prayers make us acutely aware of the cross that Jesus bore, which gives us the chance to relate to him in the shared experience of suffering.

As we explore the personal and communal aspects of Lent, we can learn new ways to approach this season. You'll come to understand the purpose behind some of the things you may have done for years without knowing how they were supposed to help get you to heaven. I hope you'll use this as inspiration to dig deeper into the season of Lent and as a starting point to explore other materials that can bring richness to these forty days.

Where's My Alleluia?

There are some significant liturgical changes in the Mass and even in the look of the Church that occur during Lent.* The altar won't be decorated with flowers; in fact, the sanctuary might look downright barren. The music will be more solemn and, incidentally, shouldn't be instrumental. Organs and other instruments should only be played in support of a vocalist. You might also notice the priest wears purple vestments during Lent, a color representing sorrow and penitence. You won't hear the *Gloria*, which is about rejoicing; but the Lenten change that

---

* For more on the liturgical changes during Lent, check out the General Instruction of the Roman Missal, paragraphs 62–63 (Alleluia), 305 (flowers), 313 (music), and 346 (purple).

I think I notice the most is the omission of the *Alleluia*. By the time of the Easter Vigil, I literally miss being able to exclaim that during Mass. And while the following isn't an official mandate, it is customary that gatherings or social activities after Mass be discouraged. Sorry kids, no matter how good you were during Mass there's no doughnuts until Easter! Many parishes have other traditions too, such as exiting Mass in complete silence during Lent.

The readings for the six Sundays in Lent reflect the solemnity of the season. During ordinary times, there is a theme that runs through all of the readings culminating with the Gospel, so they all tie together nicely. During Lent, though, the first and second readings are conveying messages about salvation and conversion, while the Gospels relay stories about turning away from sin and finding redemption. It shouldn't be a big surprise to learn that the first Sunday is the story of Jesus in the desert, which, of course, sets the tone for exactly what we are supposed to be doing in Lent.

The tone of the liturgy changes even more during the Triduum, which is the culmination of Lent. Before Holy Thursday, many churches cover the statues of saints in the church with purple cloths, which always looks particularly depressing to me. On Good Friday, there is no consecration of the Eucharist, therefore no meeting of heaven and earth. The liturgical change I dread the most is the audience participation Gospel proclaiming the Passion of Christ. It's such a stark reminder that each of us is responsible, personally, for his suffering. It is each of us, not just the people yelling in the crowd 2,000 years ago, that crucified him. We, not just they, chose to release the other prisoner. It is painful to say those words aloud and in unison with the whole Church. It's sobering to say "Crucify him" while we are looking at the crucifix behind the altar.

All of these things help increase the reverence of the season and remind us that something very sacred is occurring in our

Catholic Faith. The loss of many of our practices during the liturgy remind us of all that we gained by Jesus' passion, death, and resurrection. After all, there would never be a Eucharistic celebration without the Passion and the Resurrection! In another sense, the absence of so many liturgical staples create a void in our worship that is only filled when Christ is resurrected. Prayerfully contemplating that concept can help us realize that all the empty spaces in our lives are only truly filled by Our Lord.

#ashtag

You'll know it's Ash Wednesday when all your friends start posting selfies of their ash-smeared foreheads on social media. While it's great to show our faith publicly, it's also important that we understand why we receive ashes to begin with.

To dispel a common misconception, Ash Wednesday is not a holy day of obligation! You're not committing a sin if you don't get ashes. But maybe we shouldn't spread that around, because Ash Wednesday is one of the busiest days for Mass attendance. Although not a holy day of obligation, Ash Wednesday is a required day of fasting and abstinence. We'll talk extensively about what that means shortly, so stay tuned.

The ashes we receive are from the palms that were distributed at last year's Palm Sunday and now burnt. They remind us of our mortality, that God made us from dust and that one day our earthly bodies will return to dust. Let's face it, pondering our own death isn't exactly a fun way to spend a Wednesday, but it is important. Whether we spend eternity in heaven isn't decided by a random lottery, it's dictated by the choices we make while we're alive and the grace of God's mercy. Therefore, remembering the reality of our death can help us make better choices in life, help keep our eyes on the prize. Being reminded of our mortality also benefits the pursuit of our spiritual life on earth, especially during Lent, because it's not just about physical death. Our mortality can also remind us of the death to ourselves that's necessary to fully embrace a relationship with Christ. We have to die to our own desires to completely accept his will. Ultimately, Ash Wednesday is a rather public way to acknowledge the need to repent before it's too late.

It's crucial to keep reminding ourselves throughout Lent that we're not just participating in ritualistic habits passed down for generations. Everything we do during Lent holds specific symbolism and purpose. There's a great temptation, especially for cradle Catholics, to blow through some of these activities without much contemplation about their significance. After all, we did the same stuff last year, and we'll do it all again next year. This is exactly the reason we need to have a firm grasp on the meaning of our actions. Without understanding, this is all an exercise in repetition and won't do anything to move us toward eternal happiness with Our Lord.

Pump Up the Prayer

One of the three pillars of Lent, but perhaps the most ignored, is prayer. Obviously, we shouldn't pray only during Lent, but at this time our prayer should take on a new look. Prayer is food for our soul and is particularly important during this time of stark seriousness in our faith. As we fast and sacrifice, the devil is more than happy to amp up temptations, just like he did to Jesus when he spent forty days in the desert (yep, forty days). Prayer, which is simply communication with God, gives us strength to withstand these attacks.

What else does prayer do?

It fortifies our spirits and gives us courage, because God always answers our prayers for holiness with swift aid! He wants us to succeed at growing closer to him during Lent, so he will do everything he can to help us — even if we can't feel him working in our souls.

It gives us hope in times of desolation. In addition to the sacraments, it's our connection to heaven, which we really need to focus on during Lent. Sometimes, keeping our eyes on the prize is enough to help us overcome the temptation to cheat on our commitments.

It is critical in helping us gain a richer understanding and deeper appreciation for the sacrifice Jesus made for us. With the help of the Holy Spirit to enlighten us, we can grow in our comprehension of what Jesus endured to save us. This begins in prayer. Simply asking the Holy Spirit to help us as we read Scripture or pray will pay dividends on our Lenten journey.

Because we're called to "pray constantly" (1 Thes 5:17), it's important to be purposeful about increasing our devotion to prayer during these forty days. During Lent, I like to spend time on different prayers that I don't usually pray. I pray a lot of litanies, especially the Litany of Trust and the Litany of Humility. Search for prayers online or stop by a Catholic bookstore to get inspired.

One of my "favorite" prayer activities during Lent is to listen to the Way of the Cross from Mary's perspective. I put favorite in quotes because that word implies enjoyment. I definitely don't enjoy hearing or reading Mary's excruciating pain watching her son being tortured and killed, but I find it incredibly spiritually rewarding. It's a real wake-up call to the reality of the passion and death of Our Lord. As a mom, I can't imagine how Mary must have felt, but I think it's crucial to try to immerse myself in her perspective to help me understand the significance of the events and not take any of Christ's sacrifice for granted.

Lent is a great time to get your prayer life back on track. Perhaps you can experiment with different forms of prayer that are outside your normal habits, or maybe you need to simply begin a routine that you've been saying you would get around to starting. Make a commitment to saying a Rosary every day during Lent. Full disclosure, I did that for Lent eight years ago, and I have just keep doing it every day since! I couldn't imagine missing a day now, which is wild, because, before that Lent, I hadn't said a Rosary in, wait for it … decades! You could also try things like *lectio divina*, which is praying through Scripture or Eucharistic adoration to deepen your prayer life during Lent.

Again, there's a ton of resources available on Catholic websites and in Catholic bookstores. I recommend starting early (like, a few weeks before Ash Wednesday) to map out a prayer plan and gather resources to prepare to really devote specific time to prayer, or elevate your prayer life to a new level during Lent.

Almsgiving

We may think of the Christmas season as the most charitable time of year, but almsgiving plays a vital role in our faith journey during Lent. You may notice extra collections at Mass — it's not because the Church is trying to make an extra buck. Instead, the focus on almsgiving is to help us learn to be more charitable to those in need.

Charity is a big gospel theme for good reason. Giving money or items to those less fortunate than us directs us away from thinking only of ourselves and to think more about others. It's very easy to be selfish and contemplate our own needs and wants almost exclusively. When we shift our focus and direct our eyes outward, do you know what we see? We see our neighbor, the person we are supposed to love as we love ourselves.

Being charitable also helps us learn gratitude and humility. Charity reveals our selfishness, and we learn to be grateful because even though we may not have everything we want, we have something to share with those who have less. Almsgiving during Lent is also part of the sacrificial nature of the season. You may think that you don't have anything extra to spare, but that's the level of charity that God is calling us to during Lent. He doesn't want us to love our neighbor with our excess; God wants us to dig deeper than that and learn about sacrificial love. That's the kind of love he has for us.

Lent is also a wonderful time to go beyond dropping something in the collection plate. To truly grow in charity, we should get a bit out of our comfort zone. Try to become involved with a charitable organization. Many parishes adopt groups as part of their communal Lenten practices, so check with your parish office and see what opportunities already exist. If you can, get your whole family or a group of friends involved. Sharing the Gospel of Christ during Lent is particularly rewarding, and there's no better way than to give our time in service. By our example, we can be the hands and feet of Christ and spread his love to those who need it the most.

Last Lent, my parish adopted a homeless shelter that caters exclusively to the mentally ill of our city. Donations of all kinds of personal care items, simple luxuries like slippers and such, as well as cash for repairs and supplies, were collected across the whole parish. Additionally, we planned a day of service at the facility. Teenagers, like my son, worked with more experienced parishioners on facility cleanup and repairs. Younger kids, like my daughter, helped string curtains on rods to hang in the rooms of the residents. We all spent time making crafts and playing board games with the residents. Yes, it was a little alarming for my children to see some of this, because the residents suffered from a range of mental illnesses, some of which were fairly severe. But it was good that they stepped outside their bubble to see what other people go through on a daily basis. The day ended with a meal prepared by one of our guys who had a big, mobile cooking rig. He fried fish for everyone, with all the fixings, and after we served everyone, we sat with them and ate. If your parish doesn't have any established Lenten service project, grab some friends and do one on your own, or consult your pastor and ask if you can organize something for your parish.

It's Getting Weird

We are going to spend a big chuck of time on this next section, not only because it's the third pillar of Lent, but also because it's the most obvious and misunderstood one.

Let's face it, we Catholics do a lot of weird things. The genuflecting; the ashes on our heads; the aerobic routine of kneeling, sitting, and standing during Mass; and more seem awfully curious to others. Actually, the list of oddities could get pretty long if we think about it. While we may be incredibly aware of these uniquely Catholic things when we're with those of other faiths, it's easy to forget the two faith staples that many of us share: fasting and sacrifice.

Religions around the world practice

various forms of fasting and sacrifice. Often, they are far more stringent than Catholicism requires. Frankly, when it comes to fasting, Catholics have it much easier than our Muslim friends who actually fast from all food between sunrise and sunset for the entire month of Ramadan! And we can pick up our own Bible to see countless examples of the sacrifices that were historically required in the Jewish faith. I certainly can't imagine the congregation in my parish gathering to witness the killing of a goat.

Despite how comparatively little is required of Catholics in terms of fasting and sacrifice, I suspect most of us fall into one of four categories:

1. We don't do it.
2. We do it, reluctantly.
3. We do it, but we don't know why we do it.
4. We joyfully do it with the goal of growing more closely united to the suffering of Christ.

If I had to guess, I think Catholics who put themselves in the fourth category probably all know one another's names because there are so few in that group. I generally float around in the second category trying desperately to plunge into the fourth group. Truth be told, I spent some time in each of the first three categories at different times in my life, and maybe you have also. So, we're going to look closely at both fasting and sacrifice as parts of our Lenten journey. They have a lot in common, so some sections will apply to both while other sections will break them down individually.

The Lent Survey

A few weeks before Ash Wednesday, we feel the pressure mounting to choose our penance, which is really what our sacrifice is all about. Catholics turn into market researchers, frantically asking every Catholic they know one question: What are you giving up for Lent? Honestly, we're all going to hear similar things over and over, and we shouldn't be basing our plan on someone else's anyway. Instead of taking polls, we should be praying about this decision.

Choosing what to "give up" or, more precisely, offer as our penance for Lent should be focused on removing an obstacle in our lives that is preventing us from fully embracing Jesus. Unfortunately, we often treat our Lenten sacrifice as a second chance at our New Year's resolution.

Truly deciding on an appropriate Lenten penance requires self-examination and prayer. We have to begin by looking closely at our lives and determining where we are consistently falling short. Are we often selfish with our money and time? Do we have to repeat the same list of sins every time we go to confession? We need to pray and ask the Holy Spirit to guide us to what we should be giving up for Lent that will help us experience spiritual growth.

Anything given up, whether it is something we love that we commit to doing without or something we really need to eliminate for our spiritual well-being, is a sacrifice. Maybe it's the daily expensive cup of coffee, or perhaps it's a sin of the flesh. Whatever it is, the point of the exercise is that it's supposed to have a positive effect on our relationship with God. In other words, your sacrifice has to have a purpose. If you walk past the coffee shop and think, "I can't wait for these forty days to be over," chances are you aren't experiencing any growth in your faith life. However, if you walk past the shop and think, "Thank you, God for the comforts of my life and please help those who don't have comforts or even necessities," then you're growing in gratitude and empathy.

Second, we have to stop thinking of Easter Sunday as the end of our penance. Sure, if you've deprived yourself of your favorite morning drink for forty days, there's no harm in a celebratory cup of joe. But if you immediately slide back to your daily routine without remembering to give thanks or think about the less fortunate, then you're no different than you were on the day before Ash Wednesday. Maybe you won't continue abstaining from your pleasure, but hopefully you will partake less frequently and more thoughtfully. In other words, Lenten sacrifice should produce some permanent positive change for the rest of the year.

It's Only Twice a Year (Maybe)

When are we supposed to fast from food, and what does that entail? There are only two days out of the entire year that Catholics are required to fast: Ash Wednesday and Good Friday. Seriously, that's it. Two days out of three hundred sixty-five is all that's expected. And it's not even the type of fast that's required for certain types of medical tests! The bare minimum that's expected is that on those days we refrain from meat and only eat two small snacks and one normal meal. That's more than some people in the world get to eat every day of their lives.

Now, lest you think I'm preaching to you from my lofty pedestal about how terrible you are at fasting, it's time for my confession: I stink at fasting. I don't even normally eat three big meals a day, but the minute I realize I can't, I'm immediately starving. So, trust me, if you are bad at fasting, you're not alone. Obviously, there are some people who have medical conditions or are outside of the age bracket (18–65) that are exempt from these requirements, so I'm not fussing at you. I'm fussing at me and those of you like me who have no excuse.

You have the option, of course, to demand more of yourself than the minimum the Church asks, and many Catholics do participate in a more hard-core fasting on those two days. Some people even impose additional days of fasting upon themselves as a penance or atonement. I am applauding those people, and I hope to join their ranks one day, but for now I will just try to master the requirement!

The close relative of fasting is abstaining — not eating meat — and, again, we have it pretty easy. Pre-Vatican II Catholics abstained from meat every Friday of the year, but now it's only required during Fridays of Lent. (Still, Fridays throughout the year remain a day of penance, and some form of sacrifice is expected.) The choice of meat for Catholic abstinence is an interesting one because a lot has changed in the past thousand or so years. A lot of people now choose to never eat meat, but that wasn't historically the case. Having meat on your table was once considered a sign of wealth and prestige, which probably made it an attractive penance to be required of Catholics. But (as always!) there's also a deeper meaning considering that Christ gave his life — his flesh — for our salvation.

But Whyyy???

Everything we do in our faith is centered around the goal of getting ourselves to heaven, to spend eternity with our Father. How do we get to the Father and ultimately to heaven? Through the Son. How do we get to the Son? Well, the quick answer is to be like him. The more we become like Jesus, the more conformed we become to the ideal, the standard. In order to become like Jesus, we have to know him. We do this by reading Scripture and by spending time in front of the Blessed Sacrament and in prayer. Once we begin to know Jesus, we start to share our lives with him.

Think about someone with whom you have a very close relationship, a best friend or spouse. To become very close, you shared things. It may have started with sharing stories, meals, maybe eventually a vacation. Ultimately, to reach that next level of closeness, you had to share the hard parts of your life, the pain in your story. Those are the moments that bond us in human relationships and those are the moments that bond us in our relationship with Jesus. Of course, we have daily opportunities to share joy with God, and those moments are vital. We can walk outside and marvel at his creation, or spend time laughing with people we love, and our Creator shares our happiness with us. But by sharing in his pain, we grow closer to him in an even deeper way and can begin to become more like him.

Another reason we fast is to feel the physical effects of hunger. Hunger is a powerful thing, and the need to eat is at the core of our survival instincts. So how does hunger help us get to heaven?

- First, physical hunger serves as

a reminder of Our Lord's hunger for our souls. He desires us to be with him and hungers for us to invite him into our lives. When we are faced with the ache of an empty stomach, we should remember that those pangs pale in comparison to the deep desire the Lord has for us to give our hearts to him.

- Second, hunger reminds us to be grateful for the food we have. There are many around the world and even in our own country who feel the aches of emptiness in their stomachs each day. By fasting with these people in mind, we grow in gratitude for the ability to satisfy our needs when many cannot. Remember that fasting, like sacrifice, should change us. It's not a one and done

event; rather, it should serve
to remind us of God's children
who go without food so we can
learn generosity and humility.

- Finally, hunger reminds us
  that we rely on God to fully
  satisfy us. When we're hungry
  and eat, we will eventually be
  hungry again. God is the only
  one who can truly make us
  full, because he fills us with his
  grace and love.

Much the same can be said of penitential
sacrifice. When we give up something that
we truly enjoy, it's natural to miss it, or even
crave it. Like fasting, these sacrificial experi-
ences serve as important reminders of how
God craves our hearts. And, yes, our small
sacrifices during Lent remind us of the huge,
unfathomable sacrifice Jesus made for us
when he gave his very life. But our sacrifices
also serve in a tiny way to help us to learn to

imitate Jesus. Returning to our previous example, if we take the money we would have spent on that daily expensive coffee and donate it to a food bank, then we are truly imitating the sacrifice Jesus made for our sake.

Some of our sacrifices are chosen, while others are thrust upon us. Perhaps we sacrifice getting that new car to pay our child's tuition, or maybe we're forced to sacrifice the enjoyment of dining out because of a job loss or unexpected medical bills. Those sacrifices don't have to be meaningless if we offer them to Jesus, thereby making them penitential, but the penances we choose are different. When we choose to purposefully and thoughtfully give something up in order to unite ourselves to Jesus, we are picking up a cross; we're conscientiously grabbing the cross of sacrifice and carrying it.

Finally, when we fast or sacrifice something we love, we are making our best human attempt at making up for all the things we do wrong. We've all had the experience of messing something up and then trying to fix it. Maybe we snapped at a co-worker when we were having a bad day, so we bring them an apology bagel the next morning. Perhaps we had an argument with a spouse and dug into our position even after we realized we were actually wrong, so we cook their favorite meal the next day. That's just what we do. We screw up and then try to make it right with some action. Does that bagel really make up for snarkiness to our co-worker? No. But chances are they forgive us because the attempt to reestablish good will shows the genuineness of our apology. It's the same with Our Lord. He wants to forgive us, he yearns for our reconciliation, so he accepts our meager attempt of atonement so our relationship can continue to grow. Our Lenten efforts may be a weak attempt, but fortunately our merciful Lord gives us an "A" for effort!

But I Want It!

Some people have impressive willpower. For others, willpower is a heavy cross. Why are some of us able to resist temptations easily while others struggle to pass up something given up? I don't have any idea — that's one for God to answer. All I know is that he made each of us perfectly, and we each struggle with certain things in our lives. For some of us, the struggle against our own will for temporal wants is real and it's hard. So how do those of us who are willpower-challenged go about inserting sacrifice or fasting into our prayer lives? I have a few tips.

- Start with reasonable goals. If you know you struggle with fasting, don't try to go hard-core. Start by giving up one meal or one treat a day. Maybe you enjoy dessert every night, or a little piece of chocolate from your secret stash at your desk at work. There's probably nothing wrong with that. But if you want to start a fast, try cutting those things out for a week first as a sacrificial prim-er. Then, work up to skipping a meal or two for a day. The point is to work up to the type of fast you want to do in a way that's achievable and not in-timidating.

• Call on Mary when temptation begins. Yes, that chocolate is calling your name; I heard it, too. But you can call the Bless-ed Mother to help you resist. She will be your biggest cheerleader whenever you are trying to grow in love for her Son. She will absolutely come to your aid and help you overcome the temptation.

- If I'm attempting a tough Friday fast during Lent and the cravings are really kicking in, I do two things. First, I admit to myself that I am not *actually* starving to death, even though that's what I keep thinking (and, honestly, loudly announcing). I remind myself that I can skip a couple of meals and be just fine. Then, I look at the crucifix. There it is, the ultimate expression of sacrificial love. My momentary hunger seems to pale in comparison to looking at what he went through for me.

There's a Catch

So, you make the decision to offer a day of fasting or a Lenten sacrifice to the Lord, and you're ready to go. You know it's going to be tough, but you're up for it. That's awesome … but there's a catch. You have to do it with a smile, or at least with a clean face.

Remember, Jesus said: "And when you fast, do not look dismal, like the hypocrites, for they disfigure their faces that their fasting may be seen by men. Truly, I say to you, they have their reward. But when you fast, anoint your head and wash your face, that your fasting may not be seen by men but by your Father who is in secret; and your Father who sees in secret will reward you" (Mt 6:16–18).

Doing something for God, whether it's fasting or praying or serving, shouldn't be done so you can brag about it. We're not supposed to do these things to make other people think we're holy, because that just means we're focused on our own pride and self-image. We're attempting to gain merit before God, not rack up merit badges to display to the world. When done without fanfare, sacrifice and fasting also have a built-in humility factor that again is an imitation of Jesus. When our Savior marched to his death carrying the cross through throngs of onlookers, he didn't point people out and say, "This is for you. Hey, you over there, this is for your sin." No, he humbly and without complaint accepted the suffering and went on.

And speaking of complaining … when I loudly and repeatedly announced that I was facing certain death after skipping lunch one Friday during Lent, I really missed the mark. Jesus asks us to do penance, particularly during Lent. We agree to it out of love for him. If we complain constantly about it, is that really an act of love? For a totally hypo-thetical example, my husband enjoys going to local festivals, and I am not always a fan. If I go with him because he asked me to but then complain about it the entire time I'm there, he's not exactly going to feel the love in my actions. It doesn't mean I don't love him — and I can't emphasize that enough — but it's not being reflected in that specific behavior.

No Excuses

Every time I hear the Gospel story where Jesus says, "I desire mercy, and not sacrifice" (see Mt 12:1-8), I hear Catholics saying, "SEE! I don't have to give up anything for Lent or any other time!" But there's more to that story.

Jesus said those words in response to a specific situation. He and his disciples were walking through a field, and the guys picked some grain and ate it, because they were hungry. Harvesting grain was a sin against the Sabbath, so the Pharisees basically tried to catch them on a technicality. But Jesus rebuked the Pharisees, explaining to them that these men were not guilty of anything. He reminded them of the story of David and his companions who, because of hunger, once went to the Temple and ate the sacrificial bread. That was totally illegal in terms of Jewish law, but not in the eyes of God.

It seems like that passage might get us totally off the hook for any kind of sacrifice or fasting, but it doesn't. First, mercy is always more important than sacrifice. Going back to our coffee example, if you kick puppies and scream at people because you're having caffeine withdrawal, God would probably prefer you to grab some expresso rather than act like a jerk. Of course, this is obviously a ridiculous example, and God would prefer you not be addicted to anything, but you see where I'm going with this. Sacrifice should never be made at the expense of mercy.

Second, if we are making sacrifices or fasting, we're not doing it to obey a law. We're doing it for the other reasons we covered earlier. Finally, at the time that Jesus had this conversation with the Pharisees, he hadn't made the ultimate sacrifice known yet. He had not yet been nailed to the cross, so imitating him or uniting with him in sacrifice wasn't an option at that moment.

This passage also indicates that when it comes to following guidelines during Lent, or any other time you are engaging in sacrificial acts, Jesus wants you to use your head. If you're feeling sick or experiencing weakness or dizziness, Jesus would probably tell you to pick up the grain, or the cookie! Don't pass out in an attempt to unite to him. Remember, the goal is not to starve ourselves, but simply to allow ourselves to experience some deprivation in order to appreciate his suffering and bring ourselves closer to him. If you're feeling truly ill, eat a little something. God understands.

Give It Up and Fast

Hopefully, I've shed a little light on our weird Catholic practices of sacrifice and fasting. They're not a punishment or a method of torture. Instead, these practices are part and parcel of things we do to bring ourselves nearer to Jesus. They're a form of prayer, which is our way of communicating with our amazing Creator, who loves us more than we can comprehend. Through these particular forms of prayer, we're showing Jesus our desire to unite to him and to the suffering he experienced for us and our sinfulness. So, let's support one another in our efforts and all get to heaven.

Fasting may not be for everyone, and you should certainly consider your health, both physical and mental, before deciding to participate in a fast. But sacrifice, well, that's a different story. We can all sacrifice something. We may be able to sacrifice extras that we usually treat ourselves to, or we may not be in a position to have extras to give up. We can still give up sinful habits or give more of ourselves. We can give time, or our attention, to those around us. We all have something to offer. And the Lord sees all of it. He sees the times when we are frustrated or exhausted but still read a book to our child at bedtime. He sees the times we have received terrible news but still smile at the cashier in the store. And, yes, he sees the times we walk past the coffee shop and suffer, a tiny bit, from sacrificing our desire. He sees and he rewards us with his grace. That makes it all worth it!

Me, I love coffee. I brew a pot every morning and don't talk to anyone until I've had a cup. I am not in any way, shape, or form trying to make coffee the villain. It proved a perfect example because even the thought of me giving it up is, well, unthinkable. Hmmm, maybe I know what I should give up next Lent.

Quick Reminder:
Go to Confession!

There are two times during the year when the church strongly encourages us to receive the Sacrament of Penance — Advent and Lent. It's a great idea to start the Easter season with a clean slate, so make sure you include it in your Lenten plans. Many dioceses offer extended times for confession during Lent, so it shouldn't be too difficult to find a time that works for you.

Go for the Trifecta

Okay, I know the Holy Thursday through Easter Vigil services are called the Sacred Triduum, but I can never remember how to pronounce that word. These three days are the pinnacle of our Lenten experience. While they are not mandatory, I cannot stress enough how amazing it is to participate in all of them to finish off Lent fully! Let's break them down.

Holy Thursday Mass is celebrated in the evening after sundown and is known as the Mass of the Lord's Supper. It's the last time we get to experience the consecration of the Eucharist until the Easter Vigil. The Eucharist we receive on Good Friday is consecrated ahead of time on Holy Thursday.

Often, the Holy Thursday Mass includes a washing of the feet. Parishioners are selected in advance to approach the altar and the clergy wash their feet. This, of course, is based on the Gospel where Jesus washes the feet of the apostles right before the Passion begins, and is also when Jesus establishes the priesthood. It reminds us that we are all here for service to one another, and it's a powerful experience. The Mass ends with an invitation to spend an hour in Eucharistic Adoration (waiting one hour with Jesus as he asked his disciples to do) before the tabernacle is left empty until the Resurrection is celebrated at the Easter Vigil. If your parish has a separate adoration chapel, Jesus will be removed and the chapel closed until after the end of the Easter Vigil Mass. Additionally, earlier on Holy Thursday (sometimes it's moved to another day in Holy Week), there's another special event that you likely have never attended: the Chrism Mass. This Mass is celebrated by the bishop in each diocese and all the clergy participate. This Mass not only celebrates

Christ's institution of the priesthood, but the sacred chrism is blessed. The chrism oil is used in parishes throughout the year for the Sacraments of Baptism, Confirmation, and the Anointing of the Sick.

You won't go to Mass on **Good Friday**, because Mass isn't celebrated, but you can still go to church and receive Communion. The consecration of the Eucharist is essential to the definition of a Mass, so, since there is no consecration, there is no Mass, just a liturgical service. Whatever it is, you should definitely go! In addition to the beautiful Liturgy of the Word and distribution of the Eucharist, you get the added benefit of being immersed in this experience at or around 3:00 p.m. to coincide with the death of Our Lord. The silence at the end of the service is profound. Typically, there's time for the Veneration of the Cross, during which each person can individually venerate the crucifix with a kiss or touch.

The **Easter Vigil** is a powerful way to cap off your Lenten journey. I'm not going to sugarcoat this: it's a long Mass. There are approximately two hundred readings (not really, just a maximum of seven). You enter a dimly lit church — many parishes use candles — until the moment the Resurrection is celebrated. The lights come up and the majesty of the resurrected Lord is reflected throughout the church. *Alleluias* return, and the church feels alive once again. The symbolism is almost overwhelming. Please experience this! Now, believe me, I understand that not everyone can do the Easter Vigil, and there have been years when I've been there on Easter Sunday morning instead. If you have kids, their ages may be an obvious hindrance. For the past few years, my daughter has been in the children's choir, which sings at the 9:00 a.m. Mass on Easter morning, so staying up late the night before wasn't a great option. If you can make it work, however, it is so worth it.

It's Finally Over

I'm not talking about this book. I'm talking about Lent, the forty-day journey through the ultimate and greatest expression of self-sacrifice that our Savior endured for us — yes, you and me. The passion and death of Our Lord is personal. Because God exists outside of time, Jesus died for our personal sins as well as those souls that went before us, and those that will come after us. Let that sink in for a minute.

Now that Lent is over we can immediately revert to our old pre-Lent ways and enjoy our Alleluias, fancy coffee, and chocolate as if nothing had even happened, right? I hope not. If Lent doesn't create some lasting change, we've done it wrong. Maybe the effects won't be dramatic, but some of the spiritual growth we experienced should stick with us, if we lived the season with sincerity. Of course, there's nothing wrong with enjoying the good things we sacrificed, but they should hold a smaller place in our hearts than before. Our prayer life should not be discarded like the wrapper on a chocolate bunny. The gratitude and humility we began to experience should make us more charitable on a consistent basis. In other words, the crosses that we picked up during Lent should stay on our shoulders, but now they should feel lighter and easier to carry because we've witnessed our Savior carry his cross for us.

This doesn't mean we should carry the heaviness of Lent with us throughout the rest of the year. We can and should shed our Lenten sackcloth without losing sight of the need for constant repentance and conversion. But the end of Lent, culminating with the resurrection of Our Lord, means we get to immerse ourselves in the joy of our faith. After all, as Pope Saint John Paul II said: "Do

not abandon yourself to despair. We are an
Easter people and hallelujah is our song!"

About the Author

MICHELLE JONES SCHROEDER resides in Baton Rouge, Louisiana. She and her husband of twenty-one years are kept entertained and exhausted by their two hilarious children. After graduating from Louisiana State University, Michelle spent the first part of her professional life in marketing and management. After a few years at home with her kids, poor culinary skills led her to invent a kitchen product and start a small business. She is slightly obsessed with St. Pio of Pietrelcina and 1980s music and is involved at Our Lady of Mercy Parish in Baton Rouge.